SUPER SPRINGTIME CRAFTS

By Holly Hebert

Illustrated by Charlene Olexiewicz
Photographs by Ann Bogart

Lowell House
Juvenile
Los Angeles

CONTEMPORARY BOOKS
Chicago

Publisher: Jack Artenstein
Vice President, Juvenile Publishing: Elizabeth Amos
Director of Publishing Services: Rena Copperman
Managing Editor, Juvenile Division: Jessica Oifer
Senior Editor: Amy Downing
Art Director: Lisa-Theresa Lenthall
Typesetting and Layout: Michele Lanci-Altomare
Crafts Artist: Charlene Olexiewicz

Lowell House books can be purchased at special discounts when ordered in bulk for pre-
miums and special sales. Contact Department JH at the following address:

Lowell House Juvenile
2029 Century Park East, Suite 3290
Los Angeles, CA 90067

Library of Congress Catalog Card Number 95-26385
ISBN: 1-56565-457-9

Manufactured in the United States of America
10 9 8 7 6 5 4 3 2 1

CONTENTS

JUST HATCHED

This pair of fuzzy newborn chicks is a delightful sign that the seasons have finally changed. Make a dozen and decorate your whole house with the little hatchlings.

WHAT YOU'LL NEED

- two raw eggs
- two large yellow pom-poms (at least 2 inches in diameter)
- white glue
- scissors
- four plastic googly eyes
- orange felt
- scrap of cardboard

DIRECTIONS

1 Carefully crack the eggs by tapping them on a hard surface, like the edge of a countertop. Break the eggs in half, saving the insides to cook up for breakfast or to add in a recipe. Gently rinse out the shells with water. Set aside to dry.

2 Glue one pom-pom for the chick's body to the inside of each bottom eggshell portion. Make two caps for the chicks by trimming away some of each of the remaining top pieces of the eggshells. Set the little tops aside. Glue two movable plastic eyes near the top of each pom-pom, where the baby chick's face will be.

3 Cut two diamond shapes, less than an inch in diameter, out of a scrap of orange felt. Fold each diamond in half from corner to corner. Place a small amount of glue on two top edges as shown, and attach the beak to the chick's head, below the eyes. Allow glue to dry.

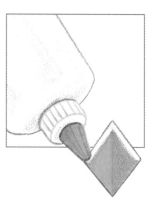

4 Cut two circles out of cardboard, each approximately 1 inch in diameter. Now cut two sets of chick feet from the orange felt. Glue the feet on top of the cardboard circles.

5 Assemble the chicks by gluing the little eggshell tops onto the chicks' heads, then glue the feet stands to the bottom of the main egg portions.

CATCH THE SPRING SPIRIT!

You can personalize your chicks further by decorating the eggshells with colorful paints and dyes.

BRIGHT-N-BOLD SPRING BASKET

Recycle tired magazine pages into a multicolored, environmentally friendly basket. Decorate your basket with a festive arrangement. Or use it to keep your things organized after an intense spring cleaning!

WHAT YOU'LL NEED

- waxed paper
- old magazine
- 16-ounce empty yogurt or cottage cheese tub
- craft glue
- scissors
- ruler
- two rubber bands

DIRECTIONS

1 Lay waxed paper over your work area to protect it from messy glue. Lay a single magazine page on a flat surface. Cut the most colorful parts of the page into triangles, no smaller than 4 inches on any one side and no bigger than 8 inches.

2 Starting with the longest side of the triangle, roll the triangle into a slender tube. The tighter the tube, the better. Put a dab of glue on the inside of the point to secure the tube closed. Starting at the base of the tub, spread glue around it. Then wrap the tube horizontally around the tub, pressing it into the glue as you wrap.

3 Make another magazine page tube. Spread more glue on the tub. Wrap the paper tube around the tub, just above (and touching) the first tube. Keep putting more glue on the tub and wrapping magazine page tubes around the tub until you reach the top. It's all right for the magazine tubes to overlap the rim of the tub. You may want to put two rubber bands around the container to hold the tubes in place while they are drying.

4 To make the handle, cut another triangle, this time from a magazine cover. (This will make the handle stronger.) One of the triangle sides needs to be 10 to 12 inches long. Roll the triangle into a tube, beginning with the longest side. Glue the handle to the inside of the tub, bending it as needed, and allow to dry.

CATCH THE SPRING SPIRIT!

Celebrate May Day, which always appears on May 1, and make a mini-magazine basket for a good friend. Using a small 8-ounce margarine tub, fill the basket with candy and other goodies. Set it on a friend's doorstep, ring the doorbell, and run—in true May Day fashion!

POT OF DOTS

Pretty spring flowers deserve better than plain old clay pots.
Turn an ordinary planting pot into a decorative container that looks
fantastic even before your seedlings sprout.

WHAT YOU'LL NEED

- newspaper
- clay planting pot
- pencil
- puff paints with writer tip, in at least four bright colors
- gardening soil
- plant or flower

DIRECTIONS

1 Line your work area with news-paper. Make sure your clay pot is clean and dry. Using a pencil, draw a design—the more simple, the better!—around your pot. You can make curlicues, write your name, or create a simple garden scene.

2 Begin your dot design along the out-side rim of the pot. Tip your pot on its side and dot a small glob of puff paint near the edge of the pot's rim. Next to it, dab a glob of paint in another color. Continue making multicolored dots around the rim of the pot, allowing one side to dry before you start on the other side.

3 Now that you've got the hang of the "dot method" of painting, make dots along the pencil line of the design you drew earlier. Fill the inside of your drawing with more, different-colored dots. When your design is completely filled in, allow it to dry.

4 Stick some gardening soil and a plant or flower in your pot of dots and gently water it. Finally, give it to your dad or mom to brighten his or her day.

CATCH THE SPRING SPIRIT!

If your "green thumb" is brown at best, your pot can double as a colorful candy dish or pencil holder.

RAINBOW STREAMER

Catch a rainbow indoors! This pastel ribbon streamer brings a fresh spring flair to any room, but remember—rainstorm not included!

WHAT YOU'LL NEED

- rubber band
- jar lid, at least 3 to 4 inches in diameter
- light-colored, pastel fabric ribbon 8½ feet long and ½ to 1 inch wide
- white glue
- eight pastel fabric ribbons, each 4 feet long and ½ to 1 inch wide, in a variety of colors
- 8-inch piece of pastel fabric ribbon, ¾ to 1 inch wide
- thumbtack

DIRECTIONS

1 Place a rubber band horizontally around the entire lid of a jar. Drape the 8½-foot-long pastel ribbon over the top of the jar lid so it hangs down on either side equally and has about an inch slack on the top to tack to the ceiling. Feed the ribbon underneath the rubber band on each side and glue down the two sides to the top of the jar.

2 Equally space the eight 4-foot-long pastel ribbons so that they hang down from the lid. Fasten one end of each ribbon to the side of the jar lid by feeding it under the rubber band. Secure it by gluing the ribbon to the side of the lid.

3 Glue the 8-inch ribbon horizontally around the edge of the jar lid, hiding the rubber band and the ends of the eight ribbons. Allow all glue to dry.

4 Ask an adult to help you hang this spring rainbow near a window or breezy walkway by securing the top ribbon to the ceiling with a thumbtack.

CATCH THE SPRING SPIRIT!

Make a Rainbow Streamer with plastic ribbons that can withstand wet springtime weather. Hang it by your front door or on your back porch to add color to the season!

*Who is watching your garden grow? The Garden Guard
will keep an eye on the plants while you're away. Plant it in the soil
of your spring crop for good luck.*

WHAT YOU'LL NEED

- stick, about 10 inches long and 1 to 2 inches wide
- stick, about 1 foot long and 2 inches wide
- two bright, contrasting colors of yarn
- scissors
- acrylic paint, in two or three colors
- paintbrushes
- four to six twigs, about 2 inches long
- white glue

DIRECTIONS

1 Look in your backyard or a park to find two sticks, one about a foot long, the second, 10 inches long. Lay the 10-inch-long stick over the larger stick, crossing it horizontally about 3½ inches from the top of the larger stick. The smaller stick will be the Garden Guard's arms. Secure sticks together by wrapping the yarn diagonally around where the two sticks cross, making an X in the middle. Keep wrapping the yarn around until the sticks are tightly bound together. Tuck the end of the yarn into the wrapped yarn and put a dab of glue on it to secure it.

2 Choose a contrasting color of yarn to wrap just around the arms of the Garden Guard. Tie the yarn around one end of an arm and wind it around the arms from one end of the stick to the other. Knot it, and again, put some glue on it. Then, using the first color of yarn once more, tie three or four loops around each arm, letting the end of the yarn dangle down about 2 inches, like fringe.

3 Paint the face of your Garden Guard. Give it two large eyes and a big, expressive mouth. Allow the paint to dry.

4 Glue twigs to the top of the larger stick for the Garden Guard's hair. Allow glue to dry. Plant your Garden Guard in the dirt. These creatures can stand alone or serve as support for tomato plants and other vine plants.

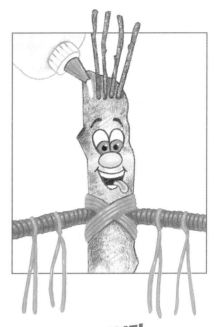

CATCH THE SPRING SPIRIT!

You can make a whole squadron of Garden Guards, each representing a type of plant. Use red yarn on your tomato Garden Guard, orange yarn on your carrot guard, and yellow yarn for the Garden Guard of your squash. Create your own color code and turn your garden into a bright spectacle year-round!

SPRING HAS SPRUNG CARD

Surprise! With the flutter of wings, an array of colorful butterflies bursts from this festive card!

WHAT YOU'LL NEED

- ruler
- pencil
- pastel-colored light-weight poster board
- scissors
- colored markers
- three different light-colored pieces of construction paper
- glitter glue
- white glue

DIRECTIONS

1 Measure and draw a rectangle, 8 inches by 12 inches, on a piece of pastel-colored poster board. Cut out the rectangle and fold it in half so the two shortest sides meet. This is the main card. With colored markers, write your friend's name on the front of the card in large, fancy letters.

2 Draw three butterflies, one on each piece of construction paper, no larger than about 3 inches long or wide. Use colored markers to decorate their wings. Give them a straight body and curly antennae. Cut out the butterflies, then add glitter glue to their wings. Set aside.

3 Cut six strips out of the construction paper (two from each color), each about ¹/₂ inch wide and 4 inches long. Place the end of one color strip over the end of a different-colored strip, forming an L, or right angle. Glue these ends together. Repeat with the other strips. Allow glue to dry.

4 Take the bottom strip of one right angle and fold it directly across, overlapping the other strip. Then take that strip and fold it directly across, overlapping the first strip. Repeat, creating an accordion-type shape. Once you reach the end of the strips, glue the ends together, pressing the folded section down until the glue dries. Repeat with the two remaining angles. You now have three paper "springs."

5 Glue one end of each spring to the back side of a colored butterfly and allow to dry. Then glue the other end somewhere inside the card. Make sure the three butterflies are spread out across the card. Allow glue to dry, then add a fun message to the inside of your card, such as "Spring Has Sprung!" or "Catch the Fever—Spring Fever!"

CATCH THE SPRING SPIRIT!

Decorate a large envelope to put your card in. Use glitter glue, colored pens, and whatever else you would like to put the recipient of this playful card in a happy mood!

TO:
Rachel

Spring Has Spring!

FIT TO BE TIE-DYED!

*Eggs are not the only item to be dyed in the spring. Turn an
ordinary cotton T-shirt into an artistic work of art.
Easy to make and supercool to wear!*

WHAT YOU'LL NEED

- rubber gloves
- three packages of fabric dye, yellow, blue, red
- two buckets of water
- plain white cotton T-shirt
- six to eight strong rubber bands
- iron and ironing board

DIRECTIONS

1 When working with dye, always wear rubber gloves. Put on the gloves to dissolve the yellow fabric dye in a bucket of water according to the directions on the package of dye.

2 Set aside the rubber gloves and lay the cotton T-shirt in front of you, front side up. Pinch a large chunk of fabric (front side only) in the very middle of the shirt between your fingers. Approximately 1½ inches from the base of the chunk of fabric, wrap a rubber band several times, twisting and rewrapping until the rubber band is tight around this piece of fabric. It should look like a ponytail. Measure 1½ inches from the first rubber band and twist another band around the fabric. Continue working down the fabric until you have three or four rubber bands in all. Repeat for the back of the shirt.

3 Put on the pair of rubber gloves again and place the T-shirt in the dye solution, according to the instructions on the package of dye. When allotted time has passed, remove the T-shirt from the dye solution and rinse it in a sink of cool water. Keep rinsing until the dye ceases to run off the fabric. Remove the rubber bands. Hang the T-shirt to dry.

4 Once it is completely dry, have a parent iron the T-shirt to help set the dye. Now you're ready to add more color. Bunch up fabric with rubber bands as you did in Step 2, except this time, place rubber bands at 2-inch distances. You'll have two or three rubber bands on each side.

5 Dump out the yellow dye from one bucket and rinse it out. Prepare blue and red dyes in two separate buckets of water, according to instructions on packages.

6 Using the blue first, rewet the entire T-shirt in cool water. Starting with the front, dip only the banded section of fabric midway between the first and second rubber bands as shown. Hold it in the blue dye for two to five minutes. Remove the T-shirt and rinse out the excess dye with cool water. *Do not remove rubber bands.*

7 Now dip the same banded section into the red dye. This time dip it in a couple of inches above the last rubber band. Soak for two to five minutes and remove. Rinse out excess red dye with cool water. Wring out all excess water. Still, do not remove rubber bands.

8 Repeat Steps 6 and 7 for the back of the shirt. Now remove all the rubber bands. Hang the T-shirt on a hanger to dry. With an adult's help, iron it to help set the colors. In your newly dyed shirt, you'll look more colorful than any Easter egg on the block!

CATCH THE SPRING SPIRIT!

Why stop with a T-shirt? Socks, sweats, shorts, and even light-colored jeans are perfect clothes to dye!

GET OUT IN NATURE MOBILE

Birds chirping, flower buds blooming, and the whisper of wind rustling through new green leaves remind us that spring is here. Bring the magic of spring indoors with a mobile you can hang anywhere!

WHAT YOU'LL NEED

- 12- to 16-inch-long branch, with a few twigs still attached
- collection of rocks, dried flowers, feathers, pine cones, seed pods, and other nature-related items
- newspaper
- craft glue
- yarn
- craft paint, many colors
- paintbrushes
- scissors
- variety of beads
- hook or thumbtack

DIRECTIONS

1 Go outside and find a branch with at least three or four twigs stemming from it. Then look for several objects from nature to hang on your mobile, such as pretty stones, feathers, pine cones, dried flowers, and so on.

2 Once you've found everything you need, take the nature items inside and place them on your newspaper-covered work area. Get out your craft paints and brushes and paint the items (except flowers) with bright colors. Try painting butterflies and other springtime symbols on a few rocks.

3 Cut several pieces of yarn ranging from 8 inches to 14 inches in length. Tie each object along various points of the yarn. Add colorful beads, too!

4 Heavier items, such as rocks, will need a spot of craft glue to help keep them in place. Wrap yarn around the object and glue on the top and bottom.

5 Tie the other end of each piece of yarn along the various twigs of your branch. Make sure the heavy items are evenly distributed along the branch so that your mobile doesn't tilt to one side.

6 To hang your mobile, cut another piece of yarn, 6 to 8 inches long, and tie it to the center of the branch. Take the other end and tie it to a hook, thumbtack, or other sturdy hanger.

CATCH THE SPRING SPIRIT!

This nature mobile will look even better with a little weekly attention. One day a week, find a 14-inch-long green vine and weave it around the twigs of the mobile. When it turns brown, just throw it away and put a new piece in. If there are no vines available, green leaves work, too.

MINI-PICNIC BASKET

Popsicle sticks become a mini-picnic basket—just the right size for having a bite to eat with friends. Load up with tasty goodies and enjoy a mini-picnic outdoors.

WHAT YOU'LL NEED

- waxed paper
- seventy Popsicle sticks (found at craft stores)
- white glue
- colored fabric ribbon, 24 inches long and ⅝ inch wide
- metallic cord, 8 inches
- wooden bead

DIRECTIONS

1 Lay a sheet of waxed paper over your work area. Glue four Popsicle sticks together in the outlined shape of a square. Sticks join only at the ends—two opposite sides lay on top and two lay on the bottom. Make twelve squares altogether.

2 Take one square and glue Popsicle sticks side by side and flat across the top of the square, leaving slight spaces between the sticks. Flip the panel over and glue two more Popsicle sticks to the underside as shown. This makes the panel, which is the bottom of the basket, stronger. Now glue together a second panel exactly like the first.

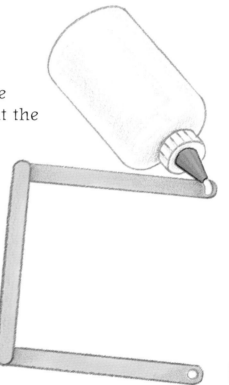

3 Stack the remaining squares on top of one another. The squares should be glued so that the top two sticks of one square are stuck to the bottom two sticks of the square above it.

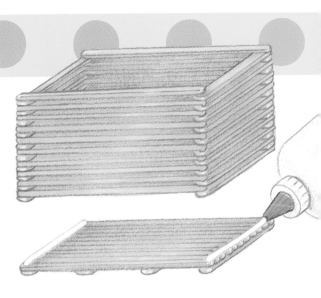

4 Glue the stack to the square panel with the reinforced side face down. The remaining square is your lid. When all glue on your basket is dry, set the lid on the basket. Snip off two lengths of ribbon, each 4 inches long. Thread one piece of ribbon near the left corner through the top stick of the basket and last stick of the lid. Tie the ribbon in a knot. Repeat this step with a second ribbon near the right corner.

5 Secure the lid by forming a loop with the cord and tying it to the top center edge of the basket. At the center edge of the lid, glue on a bead. The two should match up so the bead fits in the cord. To make a handle for easy carrying, tie a long piece of ribbon on either side of the basket.

CATCH THE SPRING SPIRIT!

Place a napkin inside your basket and fill it with crackers, cookies, or whatever tiny treats fit inside!

DINOSAURUS EASTER EGG

Where is the gigantic creature responsible for this monstrous egg?
Why, it's that amazing creative genius—you!

WHAT YOU'LL NEED

- newspaper
- scissors
- mixing bowl
- white glue
- water
- oversized balloon
- needle
- poster paint in bright colors
- paintbrushes

DIRECTIONS

1 Cover your work area with newspaper. Cut additional newspaper into strips about 1½ inches wide. Mix together 2 cups of white glue and 1½ cups of water in a big bowl.

2 Blow up a large round balloon and tie the end. Dip newspaper strips into the glue mixture, completely covering them. Remove excess glue by holding one end over the bowl and quickly running your fingers downward toward the other end.

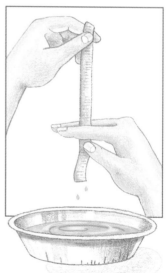

3 Wrap the strips horizontally, vertically, and diagonally around the balloon. Keep applying strips to the balloon until it is completely covered in at least two layers of paper strips. Flatten out any bubbles or bumps in the newspaper to give your egg a smooth finish.

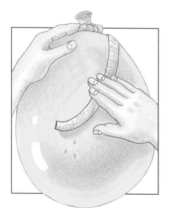

4 Clean your mixing bowl and work area. Allow the egg to dry on the newspaper overnight.

5 When the egg is completely dry, poke a needle into the papier-mâché shape, popping the balloon. If some of the newspaper on which the egg was drying sticks to it, just cut off as much as you can. Then glue down any edges that stick up.

6 Paint the whole egg in one color first. Leave a small section of the balloon unpainted so you can set it to dry. When the first coat is dry, paint the previously unpainted section the same color. Then paint a cute or zany design on your egg—colorful flowers, plaids and polka dots, or a simple striped pattern. Once the paint dries, your egg is ready for display!

CATCH THE SPRING SPIRIT!

To make an eggcellent bank, cut an inch-long strip in the top of your egg. The strip should be no more than 1/4 inch wide. Then, whenever you have spare change, drop it in the slot. (Of course, to get the money out, you'll have to crack the egg!)

FEED THE BIRDS

After the winter season, migrating birds return to blossoming trees, hungry from their long journey. Give them a snack, and while they pick, take a few minutes to look at these fascinating creatures.

WHAT YOU'LL NEED

- two heavy-duty plastic bowls, 12-ounce size
- scissors
- craft glue
- stapler
- birdseed
- hole punch
- yarn
- craft paint with writer tip

DIRECTIONS

1 Cut one plastic bowl in half. Make a glue outline in the shape of a heart on the outside of the half bowl. Fill in the outline with glue, then pour a handful of birdseed over the glue heart, covering the whole shape. Allow all the glue to dry. Tip the bird feeder over a garbage can and shake off excess seeds. The remaining seeds are left in the shape of a heart!

2 On the whole bowl, use craft paint with a writer tip to write "WELCOME, HUNGRY BIRDS!" on the top half of the inside plate rim. Allow the paint to dry.

3 Place bowls face to face as shown, and staple them together around the rim using about five staples. With an adult's help, punch two holes in the top of the bird feeder. Thread yarn in one hole and out the other.

4 Fill the waterproof feeder with seed, then tie the feeder to a tree and watch the birds come to feast!

CATCH THE SPRING SPIRIT!

Keep track of the special birds that visit your feeder. What kind of markings do they have? What size are they? What time of day do they feed? Later you can try to identify the birds that are in your own backyard by comparing your descriptions to those in an encyclopedia or bird reference book!

SOCK IT TO 'EM, BUNNY!

Here comes Peter Cottontail, hopping down the bunny trail! This soft rabbit with long, floppy ears makes an adorable prize at any springtime party.

WHAT YOU'LL NEED

- thin, white ankle-length sock, with cuff
- several jumbo cotton balls
- two buttons
- pink felt
- white embroidery floss
- needle and thread
- craft glue
- scissors

DIRECTIONS

1 Stuff the sock with cotton balls until it's filled up to the heel and base of the ankle. Tie the sock closed with a tight knot.

2 Turn the loose cuff of the sock back over the stuffed body as shown. The bunny body is complete and now it's time to add the details!

3 To make the eyes, first cut a piece of thread about 24 inches long. Thread the needle and pull about 12 inches of thread through. Knot the end, using both pieces of thread. Have an adult help you, if needed.

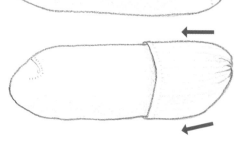

4 Sew on both eyes at the same time by following the picture shown. The needle and thread will pierce through the head, securing both buttons. Thread the needle back and forth through the button holes a few times to secure them in place. Pull the thread tight so that the head is pinched between the two buttons, giving your bunny a rabbit-shaped head. Secure with a knot and cut off excess thread.

5 With an adult's help, make the whiskers, first threading the white embroidery floss through a needle, as you did with the thread in Step 3. Tie a knot about 1 inch from the end. Now, pierce those bunny cheeks with the needle, going through to the other side as shown. Tie a double knot on the other side to secure the whiskers. Measure an inch or so of floss for the other half of the whiskers, then trim off any excess.

6 Cut two ears and a little triangle nose from the pink felt. Attach ears with the needle and thread. Glue on the nose and a fluffy cotton-ball tail.

CATCH THE SPRING SPIRIT!

Make a family of bunnies for the Easter parade. Scraps of material can be glued onto bunny bodies for vests, dresses, and any bunny accessories you'd like to add.

*Show your spring spirit by hanging a bright bouquet flag
outside the door of your room or house.*

WHAT YOU'LL NEED

- scissors
- old bedsheet
- pencil
- white paper or tracing paper
- permanent marker

- waxed paper
- fabric paints
- paintbrushes
- safety pins or thumbtacks

DIRECTIONS

1 Cut an old bedsheet into a rectangle. It can be as large or as small as you wish your flag to be.

2 With a pencil, trace each flower or leaf shown on page 32 onto a piece of white paper or tracing paper. Cut out your traced shapes.

3 To protect your work surface, place sheets of waxed paper underneath your fabric. With a permanent marker, trace around the paper shapes directly onto the fabric. Then move each cutout flower to a new spot on your flag. Trace the shape onto the fabric once more. You may trace these individ-

ual flower designs in rows or in a circle. Your flag may have lots of flowers close together or only a few. Be creative with your flag pattern—let it represent what springtime means to you and your family.

4 Now fill in the traced designs with fabric paint. Experiment with solid colors, polka dots, or stripes. Your flowers can be classic or zany—you decide. When your flag is completely colored in, lay it flat, allowing the paint to dry.

5 Tack your flag up on your door or wall as a banner, or attach safety pins to a flagpole rope and string it up the pole. Any which way, your spring spirit is displayed for all to see!

CATCH THE SPRING SPIRIT!

Get your whole neighborhood involved! Have a contest for the most creative spring flag, the silliest, the most beautiful, and whatever other categories you can think of.